STRONG

ROB KEARNEY & ERIC ROSSWOOD

ILLUSTRATED BY NIDHI CHANANI

LB

LITTLE, BROWN AND COMPANY

NEW YORK BOSTON

Rob was a **STRONG** kid.

He lifted **HEAVY** boxes, opened the **TIGHTEST** pickle jars, and always brought the groceries into the house in one trip.

In school, he tried sports that tested his strength.

He felt **MIGHTY** like an elephant as he helped pull competitors across the tug-of-war line.

He felt **STURDY** like a boulder when he guarded his team's quarterback.

And he felt **POWERFUL** like a rocket when he launched other cheerleaders high in the air.

But Rob's favorite sport was **WEIGHTLIFTING**.
It required him to use every muscle in his body.

When Rob lifted weights, he felt **TOUGH**.
He felt like a **SUPERHERO**!

When Rob was seventeen, a teacher introduced him to Strongman, a competition that tested strength in a way he had never seen before.

Competitors lifted more than just **WEIGHTS**.

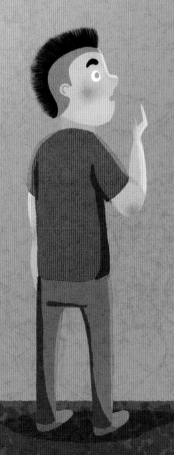

Rob entered the competition. He wanted
to be a **WEIGHTLIFTING CHAMPION**!

HEAVY
LOG

ATLAS
STONE

GIANT
TIRES

Rob was eager to begin his training, but first he needed the proper workout attire. He decided to wear what all the great strongmen wore.

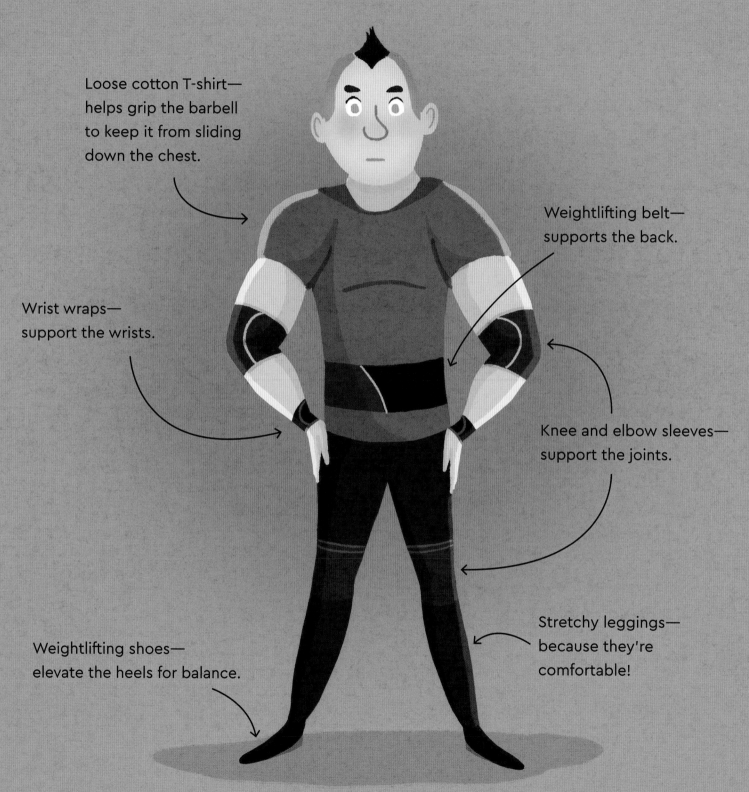

Loose cotton T-shirt—helps grip the barbell to keep it from sliding down the chest.

Weightlifting belt—supports the back.

Wrist wraps—support the wrists.

Knee and elbow sleeves—support the joints.

Weightlifting shoes—elevate the heels for balance.

Stretchy leggings—because they're comfortable!

Every day before school, when his friends were still fast asleep, Rob would **TRAIN**. He **RAN**, he **SWAM**, and he **LIFTED** weights. The different exercises helped strengthen every muscle in his body. In the beginning, he was able to lift 150 pounds above his head. Over time, that became 200, then 300, then 400 pounds! That's more than a **REFRIGERATOR**. That's more than a **PIANO**.

That's more than

**800 STUFFED
RAINBOW UNICORNS**!

That's more than **114 BIRTHDAY CAKES
WITH CHOCOLATE FROSTING AND
CONFETTI SPRINKLES**!

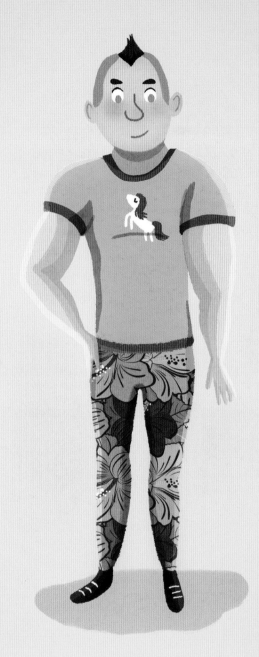

When he finished training, Rob always changed back into his regular clothes. They were more fun and expressive. They were more...him.

On the day of his first big competition, Rob strode into the event. He was muscular like all the other athletes, he wore the same weightlifting gear, and he had trained just like the champions. He was sure he was going to win.

Rob watched the other contestants lift and race their way through the challenges.

I can do this! he thought. But when it was his turn...he **STRAINED**...and he **STRUGGLED**...but he could not lift as much as everyone else.

Rob finished in last place. His feelings now matched his clothes: bleak, miserable, and gloomy.

Things started to get brighter when he met Joey at a weightlifting event. Joey was fun and kind, and he made Rob smile. The two of them **FELL IN LOVE**.

They trained together to help Rob get ready for his **BIGGEST CHALLENGE** yet: the North American championship! But after going to the gym a few times, Joey noticed that Rob always changed into boring colors when he lifted. When he asked about it, Rob simply said, "Strongmen do not wear bright, bold colors."

"But *you're* a strongman, and you wear bright, bold colors."

"But I don't want to be the only one."

"Well then," said Joey. "I'll wear bright colors **WITH YOU**."

And so he did.

Rob and Joey continued to train. In addition to weights, they lifted **ATLAS STONES**, **GIANT SANDBAGS**, and even **CARS**. One time, Rob pulled **A FIRE TRUCK** down the street!

On the day of the North American championship, Rob watched from the sidelines as the challengers sped through the course. They lifted circus dumbbells, blocks, atlas stones, and logs. He wondered if he could win. Was he fast enough? Was he strong enough?

When it was his turn, Rob stepped out onto the stage.

He wanted to hide when he heard the whispers, but it was too late. He was already on the floor, so he took a deep breath and focused on **DOING HIS BEST**.

The announcer called out, "On your mark! Get set! Go!"

But when he got to the giant log, he struggled to lift it over his head.

Everybody's looking at me, he thought.

Rob's body started to shake, and it looked like he couldn't hold on any longer. Just then, he saw a familiar face in the crowd.

Suddenly, Rob didn't feel so alone.
With one final push...

...he lifted the log over his head! The crowd cheered. Rob won the competition and was named the strongest person in North America.

From that day forward, Rob stopped worrying about what other people thought of him. Because whenever someone said he looked silly, Rob just had to remind himself of one thing.

That he looked like a champion.

Dear Reader,

Growing up, I tried to be like everyone else. I played the same sports, wore the same clothes, and acted the same way as all my friends—but none of that made me truly happy. As I got older and gained confidence, I realized that what made me different is also what made me **STRONG**. There is nothing that shows more strength than being who you truly are.

   Throughout my career as a professional strongman, I have had the pleasure of being the first and only openly gay strongman in the world. Since meeting my husband, Joey, and wearing my bright, powerful colors, I have become one of the strongest men in the world while smashing stereotypes and changing how people perceive what it means to be gay. Along the way, I have been able to bring LGBTQ+ representation to the forefront of strength sports and show everyone that sexual orientation does not define what you can achieve.

   There were many times in my life when unkind words hurt me or I thought I would never be a professional strongman. I even started to believe I shouldn't be myself or couldn't succeed. But I followed my passion, overcame doubt, and rose above bullies by being true to myself and following my heart. Today, I hope I can inspire other young athletes to live by my motto: "Train to be the person they said you would never become."

Stay **STRONG**,

R

FURTHER READING:

Websites

The World's Strongest Man, theworldsstrongestman.com

Athlete Ally, athleteally.org

You Can Play Project, youcanplayproject.org

Books

I Am Perfectly Designed by Karamo Brown with Jason "Rachel" Brown, illustrated by Anoosha Syed (Henry Holt and Co., 2019)

It's Okay to Be Different by Todd Parr (Little, Brown Books for Young Readers, 2009)

Julián Is a Mermaid by Jessica Love (Candlewick Press, 2018)

Pink Is for Boys by Robb Pearlman, illustrated by Eda Kaban (Running Press Kids, 2018)

PRIDE: The Story of Harvey Milk and the Rainbow Flag by Rob Sanders, illustrated by Steven Salerno (Random House, 2018)

Red: A Crayon's Story by Michael Hall (Greenwillow Books, 2015)

Sparkle Boy by Lesléa Newman, illustrated by Maria Mola (Lee & Low Books, 2017)

Zishe the Strongman by Robert Rubinstein, illustrated by Woody Miller (Kar-Ben Publishing, 2010)

ALL ABOUT STRONGMAN

Strongman is a sport where athletes compete in several weightlifting events that test their mental and physical strength, speed, and endurance. Some events push the competitors to see how much they can lift at one time. Other events require the competitors to move heavy weights from one place to another or as many times as they can before a clock runs out. Even though the name of the sport is Strongman, there are also women strength athletes who compete in a separate strongwoman division. Here are some, but not all, of the unique strongman events.

Atlas Stones

Named after the mythical Greek Titan, these giant spherical stones vary in size and weight. Athletes race to see who is the fastest to lift multiple stones and place them on different-leveled platforms.

Dumbbell Press

Athletes use one hand to lift a dumbbell above their heads with their arm extended straight in the air. Some competitions allow the contestants to use two hands to get the weight up to their chest before switching to one hand. The dumbbells come in various shapes and sizes for this event. Circus dumbbells have a thicker handle, making them more difficult to grip.

Keg Toss

Hercules Hold

Hercules Hold

Athletes stand in the middle of two tilting pillars for the event. Contestants hold on to chains that keep the pillars from falling over in opposite directions. The winner is the person who can hold on to the chains for the longest amount of time.

Keg Toss

Contestants throw multiple kegs (or other heavy objects like sandbags or kettlebells) over a specified height. It is common that each object being thrown increases in weight.

Log Press

In this event, athletes lift a giant log from the ground to over their heads. The log is different from a traditional barbell because it is much wider and more difficult to maneuver.

Power Stairs

Contestants race up a flight of stairs while carrying a heavy weight.

Tire Flip

The tire flip is exactly what it sounds like. Contestants flip a giant tire down a path as fast as they can until they cross the finish line.

Tire Flip

Vehicle Pull

Athletes wear a harness in this event and use a rope to pull various types of vehicles, such as monster trucks, fire trucks, tractors, trains, school buses, and even airplanes! They must pull the vehicle across the finish line in the quickest time possible.

Yoke Carry or Yoke Walk

A yoke is a large metal frame with a crossbar that rests on a person's upper back. In this event, athletes must lift the yoke and carry it over a long distance as quickly as possible. The yokes are loaded with weights. Sometimes they have heavy objects, like refrigerators, attached to them.

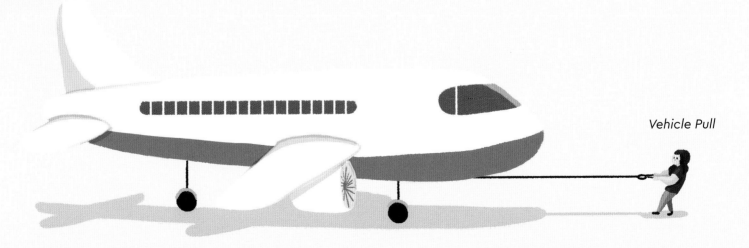

Vehicle Pull

To my husband, Joey, for all his unconditional love and always being my #1 cheerleader. To my family for their unending support—you have allowed me to be me. Finally, to the Strongman community, thank you for being so accepting. —RK

To Arree, Carole, John, Jennifer, and Lisa for helping me strengthen my writing. And above all, to my family, who make me stronger every day. —ER

For Nick and Leela, who give me strength. —NC

About This Book: The illustrations for this book were rendered in digital paint with handmade texture brushes. This book was edited by Lisa Yoskowitz and designed by Sasha Illingworth and Patrick Hulse. The production was supervised by Kimberly Stella, and the production editor was Marisa Finkelstein. The text was set in Cera PRO, and the display type is Grilled Cheese BTN.